CU00794039

ALEX BOYD is a landscape and documentary p
Outer Hebrides of Scotland. His work has b
nationally with solo exhibitions at the Scottish Parliament, as well as
group exhibitions at the Royal Academy, Royal Ulster Academy and
Royal Scottish Academy. He is best known for his collaborations with
poets, including Scotland's First Makar Edwin Morgan.

His work is held in the collections of the National Galleries of Scotland,
The Royal Photographic Society, the Royal Scottish Academy, the V&A,
and the Yale Centre for British Art in the US.

*Alex Boyd captures the natural beauty magnificently, while his studies of radar
stations and other signs of the islands' military presence, reveal another side to
this captivating place.*

THE ROYAL PHOTOGRAPHIC SOCIETY

*Alex Boyd is not afraid to document the scars, military buildings and radar
domes scattered around St Kilda, but he balances this out with images of the
archipelago's astonishing natural beauty.*

AP MAGAZINE

Alex Boyd's St Kilda: The Silent Islands *is a thought-provoking, 'warts and
all' portrait of the archipelago which pays as much attention to the islands'
brutalist military installations as it does to their precipitous cliffs and to the
picturesque abandoned houses at Village Bay.*

ROGER COX, THE SCOTSMAN

ST KILDA

THE SILENT ISLANDS

ALEX BOYD

Luath Press Limited
EDINBURGH
www.luath.co.uk

First published 2018
This edition 2019

ISBN: 978-1-913025-22-9

The paper used in this book is recyclable. It is made from
low chlorine pulps produced in a low energy, low emissions
manner from renewable forests.

Printed and bound by
Bell & Bain Ltd., Glasgow

Typeset in Baskerville by
Lachlan Young and 3btype.com

For Jessica

Prism

by Gerry Cambridge
In memory of George Mackay Brown

The tall bright arch on the black cloud –
As the squall rushes the islands,

Rattling the panes, grimacing women and men –
As the vast cloud speeds off over the sea,

Fades; and the clear light blazes round.
The seven die to the sun again.

Preface: A True Place

ST KILDA HAS A habit of both existing and not existing. The very name on English language maps seems to have been an error. Not even a strange Anglophone transliteration of the Gaelic 'Hiort' but something else entirely made from some mapmaker's imagination or lack of it.

Perhaps in Herman Melville's sense St Kilda 'is not on any map, true places never are'. And the truth of St Kilda is as complex as that of any other place.

It is to such complexity that many artists have responded over the years, and yet there is always more to do. In these photographs Alex Boyd adds another layer of visual exploration to this island group, not simply through his extraordinary ability to use the camera as a tool of aesthetic discovery but through his keen sense of the cultural and geological paradoxes of this place. Not least of those paradoxes is that St Kilda found thousands of years of continuous habitation unsustainable in the first part of the 20th century, to be replaced only by the military shift patterns of the Cold War.

It is interesting to note that Boyd's work is literally in the tradition of that great seer of cultural landscape, Fay Godwin, for many of these photographs were taken with a camera which was once in her possession. Alex Boyd is a worthy successor.

Professor Murdo Macdonald HRSA, University of Dundee

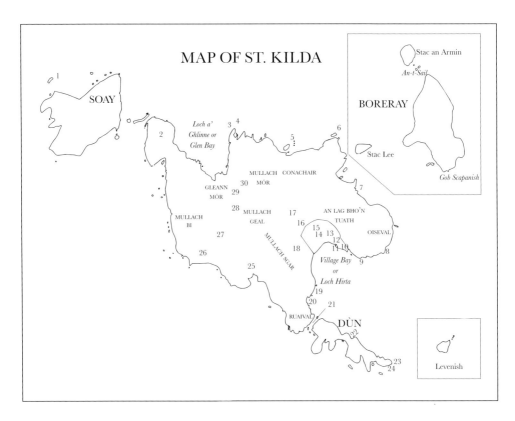

MAP OF ST. KILDA

SOAY

Loch a' Ghlinne or Glen Bay

BORERAY

Stac an Armin

An-t-Sail

Stac Lee

Gob Scapanish

MULLACH CONACHAIR
MÓR
GLEANN
MÓR
MULLACH
GEAL
AN LAG BHO'N
TUATH
MULLACH
BI
MULLACH SGAR
OISEVAL
Village Bay
or
Loch Hirta
RUAIVAL
DÙN

Levenish

1. Am Plastair
2. The Cambir
3. Gob na h-Airde
4. Geo na h-Airde
5. Bradastac
6. Mina Stac
7. The Gap
8. Rudha an Uisige
9. Point of Coll/Rudh Challa
10. Manse

11. Church
12. Pier
13. Factor's House
14. Lady Grange House
15. Graveyard
16. Amhuinn Mòr
17. Creagan Breac
18. Gearraidh Aìrd
19. Uamh Cailleach Bheag Ruaival
20. Geo Chile Briannan

21. Caolas an Duin
22. Geo na Ruideig
23. Gob an Duin
24. Gob na Muce
25. Leathaid a' Sgithoil Chaoil
26. Lover's Stone
27. Claigeann an Tigh Faire
28. Amhuinn a' Ghlinne Mhoir
29. Airidh Mhòr
30. Amazon's House

St Kilda: The Silent Islands – Tir an Airm

And there is an island in the dusk,
assured, dark, repelling,
its foundation in a fading time.
(translated from Gaelic)
– from *Islands* by Myles Campbell

STANDING BY THE QUAYSIDE in Leverburgh, a small harbour on Harris in the Outer Hebrides, I watched as tourists and crew clambered aboard the *Orca*, the vessel which would take me the 40 or so miles across the North Atlantic to St Kilda.

Making his way up the gangway, the vessel's skipper Angus Campbell looked at me with an expression of concern. Solemnly he informed me that while I could get out to the islands, it wasn't clear when I would be able to get back. I had provisions for only a couple of days on Hirta, and an incoming storm looked like it would make a safe pick-up in the next two weeks almost impossible.

With some reluctance, I decided to travel out once the weather seemed more promising. With a heavy heart I watched as the *Orca* cast off, her diesel engines rumbled into life, propelling her out of the harbour towards the distant islands beyond. So it would be many times that coming year as Atlantic storms continually battered the islands.

St Kilda had always occupied a special place in my thoughts. The islands of Boreray and Hirta, and the Stacs which tower around them, seemed impossible, immutable and unreachable, distant in their position on the edges of Europe, almost on the peripheries of the imagination.

I can still remember the first time I learned about the archipelago. I was a young boy who had only just moved to Scotland from Germany, and was discovering the country for the first time. I visited my great-uncle James in his home in Old Kilpatrick near Glasgow. Born on a farm in West Kilbride in Ayrshire in the 1920s, he had spent his life largely pursuing his favourite pursuits, such as learning Gaelic, travelling around the Scottish Islands, often on an old Clyde built steam puffer. His other great love was photography, and with his Leica camera slung over his shoulder he would meticuously document his travels, in particular a journey he made out to St Kilda with a National Trust work party in the 1960s. Fifty years later I would follow in his footsteps, making my own journey out to the islands.

On my first trip out I had the weather on my side, as well as a benevolent North Atlantic – the swell rocking the boat only enough to remind me of its presence. I thought about the story of the islands, and their now legendary evacuation in the 1930s. I quietly spent my time reading letters from the islanders to give me some insight into their plight. It was not long before the summit of Conachair, the highest point of the islands, appeared on the horizon.

My initial impressions of the archipelago were not of a lonely and forgotten outpost of the British Isles, abandoned, remote and forlorn, but of blue skies and a warm sun illuminating the cliffs of Hirta and Boreray. As our small vessel wound its way into the relatively calm waters of Village Bay, we prepared for the next

Clagan na Rusgachab, Boreray

The island of Boreray with its foreboding cliffs, towering stacs and large colony of gannets, has become one of the most recognisable images of the St Kilda archipelago.

stage of the journey, alighting from the stern into an inflatable rib which would take us to shore.

Having carefully lowered my camera cases into the boat, a task sometimes made impossible due to the rising and falling of the sea, we then set off, my eyes fixed on that most iconic of sights, the ruins of village bay beyond. It was not however the empty streets of Hirta which fascinated me, but something more modern, something absent from the countless tourist images of the islands, and much less sympathetic to the surroundings; a Cold War military base.

Instead of a structure hewn from local stone, the concrete and steel of a crumbling military installation are what first greet the eye of the visitor. Foremost among these is the unsightly but essential power station which keeps the modern St Kildans supplied with electricity, the one building which for obvious reasons rarely appears in the vast visual documentation of the islands.

Coming ashore, the extent of the military base becomes clearer, with the long low buildings of the 1960s accommodation blocks, sergeants mess, and the rather Victorian sounding 'ablution block' sitting side by side with the more well known cottages and cleits. It is in many ways an uneasy balance, but one which has allowed St Kilda to thrive, with the efforts of National Trust work parties supported by that of QinetiQ, the company who run the military base on behalf of the Ministry of Defence.

Turning my back on the base I looked out over the harbour, towards Dun, observing the strange spectacle of a bay full of yachts, tour boats and other pleasure craft. Hirta of course is a regular stopping point for a variety of cruise ships, and it is not unusual to find Village Bay thronged with tourists, wandering with guide books in hand around the ruins of the cottages, stopping to take self portraits, viewing the home and sometime prison of Lady Grange, and finishing the day by visiting the National Trust gift shop for a tea-towel or commemorative mug before boarding launches back to their ships.

Deciding to go somewhere quieter, I sought to leave Village Bay behind entirely, with the intention of exploring the lesser known areas of the island such as Gleann Mor and the Amazon's House, and to walk the ridge leading between Mullach Mor and Mullach Sgar, both hills crowned with radar stations which track live rocket firing from South Uist.

It was from the vantage point of the hills above Hirta that the island began to show a different side, with the long grassy valley of Gleann Mor offering a sense of solitude largely absent from the busy working environment of Village Bay. It was also here I began to get a sense of the knife-edge existence that those who had lived on this island must have endured, with the exposed landscapes, sheer cliff drops down to the Atlantic below, and fragile rocky promontories adding to the sense of the dramatic. It would be to this place that I would often return on my visits to the island, slowly watching mist and cloud drifting in the valley before me, concealing and then revealing the vista below.

It would be a year until I would next return to the islands, these images staying with me, the thoughts and feelings I had experienced slowly coming together in a way that made me want to respond to the environment, to document what I had seen and had felt.

I had resolved to respond in a way which did not obscure the true St Kilda. I would document the military presence as well as the natural beauty of the islands, and the ruins of Village Bay, to show a more balanced view, something which in truth is still rarely seen. I would do this all with a battered medium format camera which had once belonged to the English landscape photographer Fay Godwin, whose work I would often return to as guidance and as a point of departure.

The result is this book, a collection of images made over the course of several years and several journeys. They tell of days when the islands were bathed in a singular Hebridean light, or more likely completely obscured by clouds and mist. They are a journey around the achipelago, and are intended as a visual poem of the place rather than as a guide.

The one element missing from this book is of course the modern day St Kildans, who are forbidden to be photographed due to military secrecy laws and a reluctance on behalf of the National Trust. I hope that the voice of one of them, the archaeologist Dr Kevin Grant, may shed some light on life on the island in the beginning of the 21st century. I also hope soon to return again, to a place which is forever changing, yet never far from view, and once visited is never forgotten.

For now they are the silent islands; quietly waiting, alone out in the North Atlantic, a place of austere beauty.

Alex Boyd

Radar Station, Mullach Sgar

The Cold War landscape of Hirta, largely unknown to visitors, soon becomes apparent on arrival with radar sites towering over ridges, crowning several of the hilltops of the island.

Village Bay from the slopes of Ruabhal

The landscape of Hirta has a long history of habitation, from the Iron Age to the evacuation in 1930, to the eventual establishment of the new military base in the 1950s.

Hiort, Inhabited Archipelago

ST KILDA LIES LARGELY in the imagination. Myths and legends swirl around it like the mists which so often envelop its islands and stacs, always out of reach, always melting away and coalescing. Dimly seen behind this obscuring mist is the archipelago of Hiort, as the islands are known in Gaelic. Its main island Hirta, once home to the St Kildans, today hosts a vibrant living community of researchers, National Trust for Scotland staff, and contractors manning and operating the Ministry of Defence base which has been at the heart of life here since 1957. For over three years, I was a part of this community, and had the opportunity to observe at first-hand how the every-day of a modern working community intersects with a mythical past, the romance of isolation, and a thriving tourist trade.

To understand St Kilda today, it is necessary to consider its history. The archaeological evidence points to permanent occupation of St Kilda from at least the Iron Age, perhaps around two thousand years ago. Prior to this, we know next to nothing. Although it is a subject of much debate, most archaeologists agree that people first arrived on the islands in the Neolithic period, perhaps five or six thousand years ago. However, it is hard to say what form this human interaction took; the extremely scanty evidence could represent occasional visits, periodic episodes of seasonal or permanent occupation, or a stable community that inhabited the island for centuries or millennia. Until further evidence is found, we are unlikely to be able to say more. Certainly, St Kilda would have been a difficult place to live in earlier prehistory.

Periodic occupation was probably interspersed with periods of abandonment lasting generations.

Leaving aside the nature of St Kilda's earlier communities, an obvious question is why prehistoric people would make the dangerous journey to the islands. A good way of answering this question is to consider why the community of St Kilda in more modern times chose to live there; after all, they could have left at any time. The most obvious reason is that the archipelago has rich and varied natural resources, particularly when compared to other islands in the Hebrides. The vast quantity and variety of seabirds could be exploited, through a practice known as fowling, to provide huge amounts of food, feathers, oil and other products. These products were highly valuable in the modern period, and may have been equally in demand millennia before. The bowl-like glen on Hirte known as Village Bay provides an arc of highly fertile land, by Hebridean standards, while the hill-lands and outlying islands provide excellent grazing for animals. There would have been ample opportunities for fishing, particularly in the teeming oceans of prehistory, before industrialised fishing and whaling stripped the oceans bare. Another important advantage of St Kilda is its remoteness, which provides a degree of protection from the controlling demands of local elites. Finally, there may have been the desire to experience the unknown, to strike out toward the horizon and explore. Even as early as the Neolithic period, communities would have been confidently plying Scotland's sea-ways, working from a detailed knowledge of the sea conditions and local weather patterns that had been passed down from generation to generation. This

Bulldozer, Village Bay

A bulldozer at rest beside the helipad in Village Bay, known somewhat amusingly to defence workers as 'St Kilda International Airport'.

same desire draws many tourists to the islands today. Their sense of exploration is not diminished by the thousands of other explorers who discover the archipelago every year.

The occupation of the islands in the periods for which there is better archaeological and historical evidence is characterised by two themes: connectedness and typicality. We know that the community who lived on St Kilda came from the Hebrides as the archaeological and historical record on the islands is near-identical to that which can be found in many remote communities in the western isles. The St Kildan buildings which survive belong to a much wider vernacular tradition which extends across much of western Scotland. Christianity appears to have arrived on St Kilda at the same time, and in the same form, as the rest of the Hebrides. The same could be said of the Viking occupation of St Kilda, illustrated only through its Norse place-names. In the 18th and 19th centuries, as with all of the Western Isles, the armed forces of the British state were an important influece. The navy played a crucial role in improving the living conditions of the community in the 1860s, and two St Kildans volunteered for the British army during the Seven Years' War of the 1750s and '60s. The archipelago weathered the huge changes that have occurred across the Highlands in the past 250 years rather better than most places. There was no clearance or forced emigration, and in the 19th century its community enjoyed some of the best living conditions anywhere in the Gaelic-speaking parts of Scotland. In many ways St Kilda remains typical – the economy today is almost exactly the same as the neighbouring Uists in that its two main pillars are tourism and the Ministry of Defence.

The idea of connectedness follows naturally from an understanding that St Kilda is fairly typical. It would never have been possible for St Kilda to have been 'self-sufficient'. There is no source of stone which could be knapped to produce decent quality tools, there is no source of metal, and wood is scarce. Stocks of domesticated crops and animals need to be refreshed frequently in order to remain productive. This is why St Kilda would have been a hard place to live in earlier prehistory; the social and economic structures which would ensure regular contract with the wider Hebridean community may not yet have been in place. For the periods of St Kilda's history we know a little more about, there is ample evidence of regular visits from landowners and local elites; from at least the 16th century the island was administered as part of a group of islands which lie in the Sound of Harris. We also have evidence of emigration and immigration, with St Kildans recorded as living elsewhere in the Highlands and Islands and records of incomers to the community from the Hebrides and elsewhere, such as Glasgow. Living on St Kilda in the past meant being part of a wider social and economic system of mutual interdependence just as it does today; waiting on food arriving on the chopper from Benbecula can be an anxious experience.

The typically Hebridean way of life on St Kilda, past and present, is contrasted by the completely unique way in which it has been mythologised and captured the public imagination. There are several hundred books and papers concerning the tiny archipelago, making it one of the most written-about places on earth. A key component of the popular mythology of St Kilda

Ruined Cottage, Village Bay

It is the 1930 evacuation of Hirta, when the entire population decided to leave Village Bay to seek a new and less arduous life elsewhere, which has come to define the story of St Kilda.

is a traveller's account by Martin Martin, a Gaelic-speaking writer, later doctor, who visited the island in the 1690s. Martin's account made St Kilda a household name, and kick-started a mythology that has been developed and perpetuated, often totally independently from the reality of life on the islands, down to the present day. A key piece of evidence which suggests that the archipelago developed this split personality even before Martin Martin is its name. It is a pedant's favourite to point out that it is incorrect to render the name of the islands as 'St. Kilda'; the full stop after 'St' is incorrect as it is not a contraction of the word 'Saint'. There is no Saint Kilda, simply St Kilda. The name occurred as the result of a map-makers error, probably in the 16th or 17th centuries, and it is well attested that for many years this name was only used by outsiders. The islands have been known to the people who lived there and the wider Hebridean community as Hiort since at least the later medieval period. Most of the detailed documentary accounts describe a mythical St Kilda more than they do the real community of Hiort.

The fact that the islands were evacuated at the request of the community in 1930 is well-known, and many reasons for this depopulation have been put forward. These include the supposed inability of the St Kildans to adjust to modernity, the backwardness of the economy, a build-up of heavy metals in the soil and, memorably, vampires. It is strange that such explanations continue to be put forward – this was no mysterious event which occurred in a distant past. The evacuation was a well-documented event involving a modern, literate community whose own accounts are lost or ignored in the mass of explanations offered by outsiders. One commonality between all the reasons put forward for the 'failure' of the community is that they allow the St Kildans no agency. The possibility that a Gaelic-speaking people could make a positive economic decision regarding their future is something that has proved almost unimaginable to many writers. This is an example of a common theme in the study of Gaels, and indeed other indigenous people across the world. They are perceived as a backward people incapable of embracing change and opportunity, who need to have their best interests explained to them by a paternalistic outsider. The real reason for the evacuation was not the failure of the St Kildan way of life in the 20th century but rather the improvement of living conditions elsewhere. After the Great War, more people were being given the right to vote, living standards were rising, and the government was increasingly providing services like education and healthcare to ordinary people, services that were difficult to deliver on St Kilda. Increased connectedness and movement during the First World War allowed many in the community to observe the opportunities that were available in the wider world. In the years after the war, several families clearly felt that, perhaps for this first time, they were likely to be better off elsewhere. They made the decision to leave to seek a new, better life. Many of them found it. With the departure of so many young people, it was no longer possible to sustain those who, for various reasons, were unwilling or unable to leave. They were relocated at their own request in 1930.

The islands did not remain unoccupied for long. During the 1930s, several St Kildans returned in summer to serve the remaining tourist trade, to work their crofts, or to act as guides and gillies for

Wreck of crashed aircraft, Glen Mor

The wrecks of several WW2 aircraft are to be found on St Kilda, including a Beaufighter, a Sunderland and a Wellington bomber all lost in accidents between 1943 and 1944.

Power Station, Village Bay

Constructed in 1970, the two storey high power station houses four Mirlees Blackstone generators which provide power for the accommodation and radar sites across the island. The largest building in Village Bay, it is a structure which dominates the landscape, and for obvious reasons is generally excluded from images of the island. The low hum of the power station is sometimes the only sound heard in Village Bay at night.

the new owner, Lord Dumfries. The Second World War brought an end to this seasonal use but summer visiting began again soon after. In this period, when no St Kildans were on the islands, a vacuum existed which naturalists and geographers filled with a new set of mythologies about the islands. Independently of the wider archaeology community, they published problematic interpretations of the history and archaeology they saw around them despite being poorly equipped to do so. In 1957, the islands passed to the National Trust for Scotland and, at the same time and as part of the same process, the MOD began construction of a facility on St Kilda which was to serve as a part of the Hebrides Range. This paved the way for the way of life on the islands which continues to this day.

Since then the island has been continuously inhabited, aside from a few weeks in 2015 when it was evacuated due to a severe storm. Contractors employed by the Ministry of Defence occupy the islands all year round, mostly working four weeks on, four weeks off. Some have been doing so for 30 years. A core staff of around a dozen is supplemented by contractors and visitors in the summer, particularly when large trials at the range are planned. Alongside this core population are three National Trust for Scotland staff and a procession of researchers of various kinds, who are generally present for about six months a year. The islands' modern culture and way of life is best sampled in the Puff Inn, a now legendary 'pub' within the MOD facility into which only MOD and NTS staff and official visitors are permitted. The MOD staff comprise a mix of Hebrideans, some of whom are first-language Gaelic speakers, workers from lowland Scotland, and a small number from further afield in the UK or abroad. The atmosphere is exactly what one would expect from a working-class pub in the west of Scotland; overwhelmingly masculine and filled with robust banter interspersed with pool, darts, and light-hearted sectarianism. It made me feel immediately at home. Into this mix are the NTS staff and researchers, generally highly-educated and drawn from places far to the south. Although an unlikely mix, it works. There are many long-lasting friendships on the islands, and it is possible to have a busy and fulfilling social life there, particularly in the summer months. There have been quite a few relationships and marriages over the years, with two previous archaeologists marrying MOD staff they met in the Puff Inn. The community has its own culture and traditions, and its place-names lie alongside or replace the Gaelic names given to the islands' geography by its pre-1930 inhabitants.

There is an inherent tension between this 'native' community and the thousands of visitors and tourists who arrive on the islands every year. Given the cost and difficultly of visiting, most tourists are highly emotionally invested in their trip, having nurtured a desire to visit over years or even decades. It is one of the true privileges of living and working on St Kilda to share each day with people having one of the most memorable and happiest days of their lives, to bask in their reflected joy and sense of achievement. Most tourists spend all their time in Village Bay, the ruined buildings illustrating evocatively what they have already read and imagined about the place. Few seem aware that the majority of the historic buildings were partially rebuilt, often somewhat unsympathetically, in the '60s, '70s, and '80s. Perhaps they are happy to ignore this. For most visitors, their visit will last three or four hours, long enough for them to see what they want to see but short enough to prevent a realisation that much of the evidence on the islands stands in contrast with the accounts in the books they clutch like religious texts as they walk the hallowed ground of Village Bay.

A small minority of visitors complain, both in person and in print, about the presence of the MOD facility on the island, which they regard as ugly and noisy, an intrusion. They probably fail to appreciate that without the MOD presence since 1957 the islands would likely have been ill-used by outsiders; quite a few objects were stolen, including the church bell, in the years between 1930 and 1957. The infrastructure provided by the MOD facility allows for the tourist experience, providing water for the toilets, power for the gift shop, and a safety net during accidents and emergencies. More importantly the MOD are, more than any other group, the native inhabitants of St Kilda, and are in many ways more invested in the islands than the transient researchers and rangers. To complain about their presence on the islands and their way of life is to repeat the old idea that 'native' peoples are incapable of making good decisions about how to live their lives and manage their landscapes. It is the expensive, middle-class equivalent of Brits in Spain who complain that no one speaks English and the egg and chips taste funny. A more interesting thought experiment than considering St Kilda without the MOD is to imagine how it would be if the St Kildans had never left in 1930. Drawing on the examples of remoter communities in the Western and Northern Isles, St Kilda would be a crofting community. Barbed wire, with caught black plastic bags flapping, would stretch between the

1970s bungalows of the inhabitants. Cars and tractors would lie rusting where they broke down. It often occurs to me that the very people who most lament the tragic loss of the St Kildan community are those who would be most disapproving of their way of life had they remained.

After three years on the islands, I believe that the most precious part of St Kilda is its present-day community. It has survived for over half a century, against the odds, preserving the memories of nearly 60 years of life on the islands. There is an ever present threat that the MOD may remove their staff from the islands, funding for research and conservation alike remain precarious, and the myth itself threatens – there are many who would like to see St Kilda return to splendid isolation. I hope that this collection of images of present-day St Kilda will encourage others to value the community of people who live and work there today at least as much as the long-lost one of 1930. The best tribute to that vanished community is to ensure that the islands continue to provide a livelihood, supporting the modern Hebridean way of life. 'St Kilda' is something which outsiders bring with them to the islands. It is a reflection of their values and stereotypes, as well as perhaps their anxiety about modern life. When, at 4pm, they motor off over the horizon, they take St Kilda with them and the islands revert to Hiort, a working Hebridean landscape which is home to one of the world's most unusual present-day communities.

Dr Kevin Grant, Carlung, North Ayrshire

Workers' Accomodation Blocks, Village Bay

The accommodation which was once home to the MOD is now inhabited by the defence workers of QinetiQ. The Cold War era buildings are externally in very poor condition, having been continually battered by extreme weather conditions.

THE ISLANDS

Stac an Armin (Stac an Àrmainn) and Boreray (Boraraigh)

The 'stack of the warrior' is the highest sea stack in the British Isles, and was once home to the now extinct Great Auk. The stack has been inhabited for periods of time and contains the ruins of a bothy built by the St Kildans to provide shelter during hunting expeditions.

Stac Lee (Stac Lì)

Lying to the north east of Hirta, and only 500m from the cliffs of Boreray, Stac Lee towers above. A notoriously difficult place to land, it nevertheless has a small two person bothy, and a colony of 14,000 northern gannets for company.

Clagan na Rusgachan, An-t Sail Tower, Boreray

At 233 metres high, Clagan na Rusgachan forms part of the impressive northern profile of Boreray, the smallest of the Scottish islands to have a summit which reaches over 1,000 feet.

Stac Lee and Stac an Armin

From the south Stac Lee (left) appears to be broad, however from the west a hook-like profile is seen. Rising from the depths like a needle, like much of the archipelago the remains of a now extinct ring volcano.

Stac an Armin with Boreray behind

From August 1727 to 1728 Stac an Armin managed to support the lives of three men and eight boys from Hirta who became marooned. The 11 were later rescued, and brought back to Hirta, luckily avoided a smallpox outbreak which had broken out in their absence.

Stac an Armin and Boreray

It has been speculated that Boreray is the home of an Iron Age wheelhouse and a series of field systems. The remains of a small village on the island show that early settlers maintained an existence on this most inhospitable of locations.

Boreray from Conacair

Stac an Armin

Stac an Armin has a long history of being climbed, which continues to this day. While previously this was done solely to harvest eggs, since the late 1960s climbers such as John Morton Boyd and Dick Balharry have made ascents to the peak. Today this is rare due to the extreme difficulty of landing on the island.

Rubha an Uisge, Hirta (Hiort) and Boreray

The cliffs of Rubha an Uisge provide some protection for the waters of Village Bay, and form the lower slopes of Oisebhal, one of the highest points on Hirta. In the distance is Boreray, the second largest island some 7km away.

Geoda Clan Neill, Hirta

This sea cave is close to where the motor trawler Spinningdale was wrecked during a storm in 2008. The 14 man crew were rescued, and the wreck succesfully removed a year later with little environmental impact. Occasionally wreckage is washed ashore in Village Bay after heavy storms.

The Road to Village Bay with Dùn behind, Hirta

On the other side of Village Bay is the island of Dùn (fort), which provides protection to the bay from the prevailing south westerly wind. It is separated from Hirta by a narrow strait.

The Head Dyke, Village Bay

The head dyke, built in 1834, encloses most of the structures of Village Bay, echoing the natural ampitheatre of the location created by four of Hirta's highest peaks: Oiseval, Conachair, Mullach Mor and Mullach Sgar.

Village Bay from Clash na Bearnich

A selection of tour boats and pleasure craft moored in Village Bay. During the summer months there are many visitors to the island, weather permitting. Among these are cruise liners, and it is not un-common to find Hirta thronged with tourists. This explains the presence of a National Trust gift shop located near the harbour.

Cleitan, Village Bay

Aside from the ruins of homes in Village Bay, it is the cleitan which have come to be some of the most well known structures on the island. This is perhaps unsurprising given that there are 1,200 of them throughout the archipelago, once used for the storage of peats, grain and food. It is thought that the cleitan emerged in the late medieval period, and were in continual usage until the 1930s.

Stone wall and Oiseval from Village Bay

The stone walls of Village Bay show the effects of hundreds of years of weathering, and attempts at maintenance and repair, from the elements on Hirta, which is one of the most exposed locations in the British Isles. Behind the peak of Oiseval looms over the settlement.

Head Dyke with Conachair behind

Conachair is the highest point of St Kilda, with its peak some 430 metres above sea level. From its summit, the highest sea cliffs in Britain plunge directly down to the Atlantic below.

Ruined cottages, Village Bay

The abandoned cottages of St Kilda are one of the most obvious reminders of the evacuation of the island in 1930. Many have been restored by National Trust work parties, returning them to their original condition. One such example houses a museum, while others serve as accommodation for National Trust volunteers.

Conachair from Village Bay

The street and ruins of Village Bay are kept in good condition due to the efforts of the National Trust who work dilligently throughout the year to maintain them. There are the remains of some 30 blackhouses on the island, the result of a visit from Sir Thomas Dyke Ackland, who found the earlier settlement to be primitive, and donated money to their construction to improve the lives of the islanders.

Cemetery Wall, Village Bay

The cemetery in Village Bay predates the modern village, with walls which have been reconstructed several times throughout its history. Roughly oval in construction, the cemetery contains the remains of several hundred St Kildans and has probably been the site of burials for at least 1,000 years.

Village Bay and Oiseval

The long street of Village Bay showing the ruins of the blackhouses built in the 1830s to replace the earlier village which does not survive. The blackhouses were excellently suited to the environment, perhaps more so than the cottages built in the 1860s.

Restored Cottages and Museum, Village Bay

The cottages of Village Bay, abandoned during the evcuation of 1930, were left to decay until restoration work began in the 1960s. This began with House Number One in 1964, and was part of a wider effort to provide more permanent lodgings for the NTS staff stationed on Hirta.

Restored Cottage, Village Bay

In the late 1950s National Trust for Scotland work parties began to arrive on the island, tidying up collapsed walls, making repairs to the street and carrying out other basic forms of conservation work. There are 16 cottages in Village Bay which form a gentle arc known as The Street. The majority remain in a state of ruin.

View to Dùn, Village Bay

A view to the island of Dùn from inside one of the ruined blackhouse cottages. This home remains open to the elements, its contents long since removed during the evacuation and subsequently by National Trust for Scotland work parties.

The Store, Village Bay

The Tacksman's House, originally believed to have been built some time in the 1790s, has been used for a variety of purposes, from a place to hold church services, to a storehouse for goods produced on the island. During the First World War the store was shelled and damaged by a U-boat which had come to destroy a Royal Naval signal station. In response a gun emplacement was installed to protect the village. Today the building is used as a bothy.

Ship's bell of the HMAV *Aghelia*, Village Bay

The bell of the Aghelia, *a landing craft of the British Army which used to supply the military base during the 1960s. Designed to carry 350 tonnes of supplies, the role of these ships has now largely been replaced by helicopters. The journey to and from supply bases on the Scottish mainland onboard these vessels was noted for being not only slow, but also arduous for crews and passengers.*

Cemetery wall, Village Bay

The cemetery on Hirta, with its circular enclosure, is one of the most recognisable features in Village Bay. The wall stands on the site of much older structures, including that of a medieval chapel which had fallen into disrepair by the mid-18th century.

Cemetery wall, Village Bay

The construction of the cemetery wall began sometime between 1830 and 1844. The island's Reverend Neil Mackenzie took an active role in the building of the wall, having buried three of his own children lost in infancy in the graveyard.

Cemetery, Village Bay

The impressive tombstone in this image commemorates not a St Kildan, but that of Magaret Mackay, sister of the island's minister. A native of Jeantown (an old name for Lochcarron village on the Scottish Mainland), Magaret died in the Manse in 1874.

Head Dyke wall, Village Bay

Mullach Sgar, Village Bay

The walls of Village Bay contain stones looted from previous structures, with the evidence of several previous head dykes, cleitan and chapels all contained within them.

Mullach Mór and Conachair

The Factor's House, Village Bay

The Factor's House was constructed in the 1860s for Norman MacRaild, factor to Sir John Macpherson MacLeod. The building, of a simple design, has accommodated visitors to the island, such as photographers, and was once home to the island's warden and visiting researchers.

Cleitan along the gap between Conachair and Oiseval

This route up to the gap has long been a favourite for those visiting the island as the view to Boreray is one of the finest on Hirta.

Romney Hut, Village Bay

This large hut, part of the Cold War base in Village Bay, was primarily used as a recreation and sports hall. It was destroyed during a heavy storm a couple of years ago and has now been entirely removed.

Fuel storage tanks, Village Bay

Located beside the helicopter landing pad are nine identical oil storage tanks, part of the fuel depot which supplies the military base on Hirta.

Wind monitoring station, Village Bay

Located near the helicopter pad, or 'St Kilda International Airport' as it is amusingly known, this wind monitoring station has recorded some of the most extreme weather in the UK. Due to its exposed location, it is not uncommon for St Kilda to have more than 70 days a year with gale force winds, one year a windspeed of 144 miles per hour was measured here.

Skull of Soay sheep, Village Bay

The sheep of St Kilda are believed to be some of the earliest survivors of a neolithic breed, first brought to the island of Soay in the Neolithic period. These feral sheep which now roam free throughout Village Bay were established there after the evacuation in 1930 and are the subject of intense study by international scientists.

Abhainn Ilishgil, view to Mullach Mór

The river which runs through Village Bay passes directly under the head dyke, and is one of several rivers to be found on the island. Its name translates as 'deep stream of the spring' or alternatively 'shining stream in the gully'.

Military Road to Mullach Mór

It is a persistent falsehood that the military roads leading from Village Bay to the radar tracking stations on Mullach Mor were built from the abandoned ruins of the settlement. In reality the MOD and the National Trust for Scotland worked together from the beginning to conserve what was left of Village Bay, establishing a new quarry above the village at Creagan Breac.

Detail of enclosure, An Lag Bho'n Tuath

The enclosures of An Lag Bho'n Tuath are nestled in the hollow leading up to the gap, a wide pass between Oiseval and Conachair. The ground here was suitable for summer grazing as well as growing food for the long winters on Hirta.

Cliffs of Oiseval

The steep cliffs of Oiseval drop some 300 metres to the Atlantic below. Incredibly sheep still graze on some of the ledges which were long ago abandoned by islanders, the remains of cleitan often perilously close to the precipice. It is from these cliffs that St Kildan cragsmen descended to catch food and later to demonstrate their skills to tourists.

The enclosures on the floor of An Lag Bho'n Tuath

The valley of An Lag Bho'n Tuath and the slopes of Conachair provided the population of Hirta with rich supplies of peat and turf for their fires.

Road to Mullach Mór

Through negotiation, the route of the military road was planned to provide as little damage to Village Bay as possible, avoiding the main structures and instead passing through the lower crofts. Although much of the 19th century farming areas were damaged, this solution was seen as the best way to conserve more important locations on the island.

Radar installation, Mullach Mór

The radar installations of Hirta where constructed primarily with the aim of tracking launches from the missile bases in South Uist. The facilities are equipped to monitor these launches, with the seas between Uist and St Kilda being used to test the first guided nuclear weapon, the Corporal Missile, in the early 1960s.

Radar installations on Mullach Mór

The Decca radar stations on Hirta have the capability to photograph launches and are now managed by a civilian company, QinetiQ, who continue to monitor launches from the mainland. The large telemetry mast was installed in the 1980s and is visible from much of Hirta.

Mist on the road to Mullach Mór

The weather on St Kilda is notoriously changeable, with thick mist often descending quickly on the hill tops around Village Bay and obscuring everything in moments. The road is lined on both sides with cleitan.

Radar Installation, Mullach Mór

The radar installations were constructed by airmen of the RAF (5004 Airfield Construction Squadron) between 1957 and 1958 using bulldozers and other heavy equipment. Visible in this image is the message 'Welcome to St Kilda', viewable to approaching helicopters as they make their way to the helipad in Village Bay below.

Radar installation, Mullach Mór

While the military presence on Hirta will remain for the near future, eventually all physical signs of the base will be removed, in a process that the National Trust have already begun in co-operation with the MOD.

View to Oiseval from Ruabhal

The view looking east to Oiseval (whose name literally translates as 'The Eastern Hill'). This image clearly shows the steep wall which climbs up from Village Bay to the summit, used to stop cattle and other livestock from getting too close to the cliffs.

Mullach Sgar Radar Installation, St Kilda

The domes of Radar Stations will be familiar to many Scots who grew up in or lived through the Cold War. In the Outer Hebrides in places such as St Kilda and Uist, they are a constant reminder of the continuation of Britain's role as a major arms developer.

Weather Station, Ruabhal

This telemetry station on the slopes of Ruabhal provides important data on windspeed and direction, helping to send information back to the mainland as to whether or not safe landings can be made on the island.

Navigation Equipment, Ruabhal

This curious looking object is part of the navigation system to help ships safely enter Village Bay. In the distance Stac Levenish (Leibhinis) is visible, part of the rim of the ancient volcano which included Ruibhal, Dun and Mullach Sgar.

Dun from Mullach Sgar

The slopes of Mullach Sgar provided arable land to the St Kildans, something we can see in the landscape today with evidence of feannagan (lazy beds) and their distinctive ridge and furrow features.

Village Bay from Ruabhal

Looking down to Village Bay, the conservation area of the island, the prominent structures such as the round walls of the cemetry and the long line of the street become most apparent.

Gleann Mhór

Gleann Mhór's earliest structures date to the late medieval period, with the remains of habitation scattered across the valley floor. On the north side of the island, the Glen, which forms a natural ampitheatre, mirrors that of Village Bay and has long been used as a place of pasture on Hirta.

Gleann Mhór looking up to the radar installation on Mullach Mhór

The slopes of Mullach Mhór rise steeply from the valley floor of Gleann Mhór up to a height of 361 metres.

Wreckage of Short Sunderland ML858, Gleann Mhór

While unoccupied during the Second World War, the conflict did manage to reach the shores of St Kilda, unsurprising given its position in the key battleground of the North Atlantic. This aircraft was lost on a navigation exercise on 7 June 1944, with the loss of ten crew: six New Zealanders, three Britons and an Australian.

Cleitan and road to Gleann Mhór, with Soay behind

The island of Soay (Soaigh in Gaelic) takes its name from the Norse, translating as 'Island of the Sheep', a fitting title as it is home to one of the oldest known breeds of sheep. A steep mountain peak rising from the seabed below, Soay is separated from Hirta by a narrow 500m channel and, like many of the islands in the archipelago, is only landed with great difficulty. It is believed that Soay has never been permanently occupied.

Cleit in Gleann Mhór

Entrance to the natural spring, Gleann Mhór

Towards the seaward end of Gleann Mhór lies the freshwater spring of Tobar Nam Buaidh (Well of the Virtues or of the Excellent Qualities). Wells such as these were often associated with the ability to cure those with ailments, with this example being said to cure deafness and nervous diseases.

Cleitan of Gleann Mhór

Mina Stac, below the cliffs of Conachair

Mina Stac stands an impressive 61 metres above the Atlantic, but it is completely dwarfed by the cliffs of Conachair which tower overhead.

Wall, Gob na h-Airde

This wall at the end of Gob na h-Airde is at the end of the steep promintory in Glen Mor and is the entrance to the substantial sea cave which cuts under the headland below.

Conachair and Geo na h-Airde sea cave from Gob na h-Aird

The sea cave of Geo na h-Airde is one of the largest on Hirta and passes completely under the headland. Home to seals whose barking echoes throughout the cave, it can be accessed by climbing down its western side, proving one of the more memorable experiences on the island.

Cleitan with Ruabhal behind

Cleitan, Claigeann an Tigh Faire

Cleitan, Mullach Sgar

169

Leathaid A' Sgithoil Chaoil

Mullach Sgar, view to Claigeann an Tigh Faire

The name Claigeann an Tigh Faire translates as 'Skull of the Watchhouse', the reason for which becomes apparent when studying the shapes and forms of this rock outcrop, seen here slowly emerging from the mists.

Claigeann an Tigh Faire

According to an account written in 1928 by a Mathieson, this series of cleits around the 'Skull' were once a watch house, manned day and night. They stand on the steep ridge leading up to the peak of Mullach Bi, and have a commanding view of the valley floor below.

The Lover's Stone

The Lover's stone, with its precarious drop over a precipice to the crashing waves of the Atlantic below, is a place associated with many myths and legends. It is a site which shares many stories with that of the Mistress Stone, located nearby.

The Mistress Stone

First published in 1698, Martin Martin's account of a journey to St Kilda mentioned the Mistress Stone as a place where '…every Bachelor-wooer is by an ancient custom obliged in honour to give a specimen of his affection for the love of his mistress'. This custom required the suitor to stand one-legged and peer over the edge to the abyss below, marking him out as worthy of any woman. Whether this custom was entirely invented by the locals to amusingly mislead Martin or whether it has its roots in reality have yet to be ascertained.

Cleitann, Clais na Bearnach

Clais na Bearnach lies on the west side of Village Bay and has been the site of many discoveries from the prehistoric era, including pottery and tools.

Clais na Bearnach, Ruabhal

This site contains the former remains of St Brianan's Church, a chapel written about during the time of Martin Martin's visit to the island in 1698. Today nothing remains of this early structure. Close by is Uamh Cailleach (The Cave of the Old Woman) which takes its name from the legend of Fearchar and Dugan. These two men visited the island, terrorised the inhabitants, and an old woman hid within this cave to escape them, later emerging to identify the criminals.

Cul Cleite, Dùn

Cul Cleite is the exposed headland at the north western end of the island of Dùn. Facing the prevailing south westerly Atlantic winds, it provides some shelter to Village Bay.

Dùn from Ruabhal

The island of Dùn is separated from the rest of Hirta by Caolas an Dùin (The Straits of Dùn), a narrow channel which was once bridged by a sea arch. A local legend holds that the arch was destroyed in a collision with a galleon of the Spanish Armada. In reality it is more likely that it collapsed during a storm.

Mullach Bi from Ruabhal

The precipitous cliffs of Mullach Bi, which reach a height of 358m. On its grassy slopes is the location of at least one bothy, which is reached by way of a difficult descent from the cliff edge above.

Dùn and Ruabhal in the mist

'The work of the eyes is done.
Go now and do the heart-work
on the images within you'

Rainer Maria Rilke

Acknowledgements

I would like to thank the following people for their support and encouragement in the making of this book.

Dr Kevin Grant for his insightful essay and early support of the project, Murdo Macdonald for his kind preface, Lachlan Young for his dedication, patience and expertise in bringing this book together, Gerry Cambridge for his continued support, friendship and fine poetry. Thanks also to The National Trust for Scotland, Myles Campbell, Mary Smith, Dr Robert MacFarlane for his enthusiasm, the team at An Lanntair, in particular Roddy Murray, Jon Macleod and Elly Fletcher. Thanks to Fay Godwin, Angus Campbell at Kilda Cruises, and the team at Luath, especially Gavin MacDougall. Thanks also to Stuart, Jeannie and Pamela Bell for their support. Finally I'd like to save special thanks to Jessica without whose support, friendship and love that this project would have never left the darkroom. This book is dedicated to her.